There is a Season

For Murphy, Ada and Bucky, thank you for showing me the joy in each season.

There is a Season is a uclanpublishing book

First published in Great Britain in 2024 by
uclanpublishing
University of Central Lancashire
Preston, PR1 2HE, UK

Text and illustrations copyright © Kerri Cunningham, 2024

978-1-916747-10-4

3 5 7 9 10 8 6 4 2

The right of Kerri Cunningham to be identified as the author and illustrator of this work has been asserted in accordance with the Copyright, Designs and Patents Act 1988.

All rights reserved. No part of this publication may be reproduced, stored in a retrieval system, or transmitted in any form or by any means, electronic, mechanical, photocopying, recording or otherwise, without the prior permission of the publishers.

A CIP catalogue record for this book is available from the British Library.

Printed and bound in Great Britain by Page Bros Ltd.

Murphy's Sketches

There is a Season

 uclanpublishing

✭ ✭ ✭ SEASON'S GREETINGS! ✭ ✭ ✭

The year is split into four seasons: spring, summer, autumn and winter.

As the year moves through these seasons, there is lots to see and do.

There is a season to match all moods with different food to taste, different clothes to wear, different sounds to hear, different things to enjoy and many different sorts of adventures to be had.

The same places you might see every day can change so much it feels like you're in another world, and there is lots and lots to explore.

Each season is special and each one is lovely in its own way. A bit like us!

When you read through all these poems, you might think of lots of things you love about each season, and you might discover some new things to love about each one too.

You could even have a go at writing a poem yourself about your favourite season. You don't have to be the best at spelling, and you don't even have to make it rhyme. It can be a lot of fun to write poems. You could make a list of all your favourite things about the seasons and draw some pictures to go along with it.

DID YOU KNOW…
* There are 4 seasons: spring, summer, autumn and winter.

* Each season is made up of 3 months of the year.

* Each season is different. They have different types of weather, different days that people celebrate and different sorts of plants and flowers that bloom and grow.

Enjoy exploring the world around you.

Love from,
Kerri x

IN SPRING

In spring, nature puts on quite a show,
Trees bloom pink and flowers grow.
And that's why it's so fun to go
And get outside in spring.

In spring, there can be April showers.
All of that rain is great for flowers!
It's lots of fun to pass the hours
Jumping in puddles in spring.

Spring babies are so sweet,
Little chicks with orange feet.
Take a trip to go and meet
New arrivals in the spring.

PLANT A GARDEN

Plant a garden,
Watch it grow.
Have some patience,
Growth is slow.
But it's worth it,
You will know,
When you see your garden start to grow.

PUDDLE JUMPING

It doesn't get much better,
When the weather's getting wetter,
Than pulling on your boots,
And running from your door.

"Go and grab your coat,
Or do you need a boat?"
That is a lot of puddles,
That are strewn across the floor!

You take a great big leap,
And down come both your feet.
A satisfying splash,
And there's water everywhere!

Now your socks are soaking wet,
And you happened to forget
Your hat and your umbrella,
So there's water in your hair!

RAINBOW

Ready for all sorts of weather.
Adventures to be had.
In springtime,
New life grows.
Beautiful blooming flowers,
On green trees.
We see a rainbow.

LITTLE LAMBS

Little lambs are leaping,
Through lush green fields.
Running by their mothers,
And jumping in the air.

Fluffy little clouds,
of white and black and grey.
When you pass by fields in springtime,
You see them everywhere.

These playful little babies,
So new to the world.
Underneath the blue skies,
They skip without
a care.

SPRING FLOWERS

First the snow drops say, "Hello",
Then the yellow and purple crocuses grow.
Rows of daffodils tall and bright,
Yellow and orange; a sunshine delight.
The hyacinths white, pink and blue,
Then beautiful tulips peeking through.
Spring flowers growing all around,
A carpet of colourful blooms on the ground.

THE EGG HUNT

You follow a trail through the garden,
Where will the treasure be found?

You carry your basket with great care,
And keep your keen eyes on the ground!

Searching for flashes of shimmering foil,
Hiding amongst the grass.

And then finally you spot
One inside a flower pot,
And you cry, "I've found one at last!"

THINGS TO SEE IN SPRING

Daffodils

Lambs

A rainbow

Tadpoles

Blossom trees

Birds nesting

THINGS TO DO IN SPRING

Make a spring nature hunt and get outside.

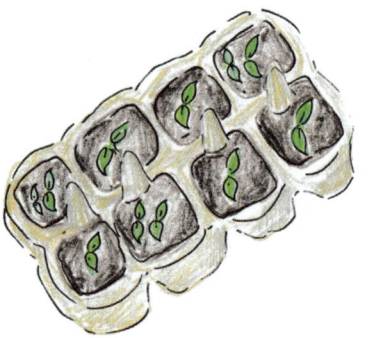

Plant something and watch it grow.

Splash in puddles wearing your wellies.

Feed the ducks.

Take a trip to a farm to see some baby animals.

Make some spring crafts like a rainbow painting or a bird feeder.

SPRING DAYS

EASTER – a christian festival to celebrate the resurrection of Jesus.

HOLI – the festival of colours. A Hindu festival, to celebrate good triumphing over evil.

PASSOVER – a Jewish festival.

THE BEACH

Staring out of our windows,
And then we see sand dunes.
We shout, "Hurray, it's time to play,
We're going to be there soon!"
We bundle out of our car,
We're off to find a good spot.
With wind breakers, picnic blanket,
And a parasol in case it gets hot.
Then when we've set up camp,
We run across the sand.
We dip our toes, as the breeze blows,

And laugh whilst holding hands.
We head back for our buckets,
And we fill them with our spades.
Then stand back and admire
The castle that we've made.
We search the shore for treasure,
Some shells and shiny stones.
We inspect them and then put them back,
Safe in their sandy home.
After many fun-filled hours
The sun is starting to set.
So much glee, beside the sea,
Memories we'll never forget.

A TRANSFORMATION

Little black specks
On a tiny green leaf.
Then little bite marks,
Made with something like teeth.
Getting bigger and bigger,
Chomping leaves all day.
Then after a few weeks
It's time to make their way
To a chrysalis home,
Where they'll stay for a while
And when they emerge
They'll do it in style!
So many colours
On their papery wings,
From a green caterpillar
Comes such colourful things.
How lovely it must be
To suddenly fly.
When their wings dry off,
They take to the sky!

SUMMER

Summer is hazy orange hues,
The familiar smell of barbeques.
It's crickets chirping in long wavy grass,
And lying back to watch clouds pass.

Summer is carefully dipping a toe
In fizzling foam as waves to and fro.
It's picking a place to perch in the sand,
And sitting together while holding hands.

Summer is sunshine, long friend-filled days,
 Imagining all sorts of games to play.
It's licking ice lollies and eating ice cream.
The flowers will grow and the grass is green.

A PICNIC FOR YOU AND ME

Let's pack a picnic for you and me,
Some sandwiches and a flask of tea.
We'll sit beneath a blossom tree,
And be as happy as can be
On our picnic for you and me.

TINY SEASIDE WORLD
(a haiku)

Beside the seaside
You can see pools of water
Filled with tiny worlds.

THE BUSY BEE

A little honey bee
Buzzes by so busily.
But what is it she does,
Except fly by and buzz?
Bees do an awful lot,
Much more than fill a honey pot.
(Which by the way has healing powers.)
They pollinate the crops and flowers.
Without bees we'd lose our crops.
The work they do just never stops.
We cannot let their species end,
We must protect our buzzy friends!
So if you see them buzzing by,
Don't you fret just let
　them fly.
They're just busy passing
　through,
Having important
　work to do.

THE MEADOW

Flutters of yellow and white
Sway in the soft summer breeze.
Sunlight turns green grass golden,
And it shimmers like waves of the sea.
Sparkling as they move together – alive,
Under the bright blue sky.
Grasshoppers hop and butterflies dance
Across the meadow.

THINGS TO SEE IN SUMMER

A butterfly

A dandelion clock

Shells

A ladybird

A bee

Wild flowers

THINGS TO DO IN SUMMER

Eat an ice cream.

Take a trip
to the beach.

Make a daisy chain.

Go fruit picking.

Blow bubbles.

Have a picnic.

SUMMER WORDS

Sunny

Beach

Bubble

Holidays

Picnic

Butterfly

SUMMER DAYS

THE SUMMER SOLSTICE – the longest day of the year. This is celebrated in different ways across the world including the Wianki festival in Poland.

DRAGON BOAT FESTIVAL – a holiday celebrated in China. They celebrate by racing dragonboats and eating a traditional food called zongzi. It takes place in May or June.

WIMBLEDON – an annual tennis tournament held famously at Wimbledon in England.

WHEN AUTUMN COMES CALLING

When autumn comes calling
It brings all sorts of yummy stuff.
Like hot chocolate with marshmallows,
Topped with cream whipped into fluff.
Big bowls of wholesome soup,
That will warm you to your core.
With thick slices of delicious bread
So tasty you'll want more.
Pastries topped with cinnamon,
Straight from the oven and hot!
Healthy harvest vegetables,
All cooked up in a pot.
So when autumn comes calling,
Make sure you grab a spoon.
Yummy food to fill your tummy
Is on its way very soon.

THE PERFECT DAY TO FLY A KITE

We're waiting for the perfect day
To go and fly our kite.
We can't go out just any day,
It's got to be just right.
Then one morning we open the curtains,
And there are leaves blowing all around,
And when we listen we can hear it,
The rush of a blustering sound.
We shout, "Finally, it's here!
It's the perfect day!"

We grab our kite and fetch our coats,
And now we're on our way,
Off to the park we go!
We take turns so it's fair —
To run as fast as we can,
And throw the kite up in the air.
It isn't easy at first,
It takes a while to get it right.
But then all of a sudden off it soars,
And we have to hold on tight.
It dances high above us,
And we look up and laugh with glee.
The perfect day to fly a kite,
Together you and me.

FROM TINY ACORNS

A tiny little acorn
Sitting high up in the tree.
Feeling snug as a bug,
Just as comfy as can be.
Watching other acorns fall,
And asking where are they going?
As they pass by they shout, "Hello,
It's time to get growing!"
And the tiny little acorn thinks,
"No thanks that's not for me.
I'd rather stay here comfortable,
And cosy in my tree."
One day something's different,
It's time for the acorn to fall,
But living down on the ground
Doesn't appeal very much at all.
"I'm just a tiny acorn,
And I don't want to go."
Don't worry little seed what
   you don't yet know,
Is from the tiniest of acorns,
   the mighty oak trees grow!

One day you'll have branches,
Filled with acorns of your own.
And you'll stand tall, so proud,
To be their comfy home.

I SEE AUTUMN

I see autumn in technicolour,
It's made of many hues:
Golden sunsets, pinkish mornings,
And crisp clear skies of blue.

I see autumn in technicolour,
The trees seem to change every day.
They rain down a colourful carpet of leaves
As their branches rustle and sway.

I see autumn in technicolour,
Crystal cobwebs laced up white.
Dew droplets hanging from each tiny line
That glisten and gleam in the light.

I see autumn in technicolour,
The most beautiful season of all.
The sunset, the dew drops, the clear sky,
And the show the leaves make as they fall.

A POEM FOR A COSY DAY

I don't really mind
If the sun doesn't shine,
That doesn't much matter to me.
Cuddled up close
On the sofa with toast,
There's no better place to be.

A movie or two,
And books – quite a few!
Perhaps a tasty treat.
A cuppa for you
And one for me too.
These days, they can't be beat.

Tomorrow it may be
A sunnier day.
Let's just wait and see.
Today let's just stay
All cosy this way,
You snuggled up here
   with me.

BONFIRE NIGHT
(a haiku)

It sounds like thunder,
We stand looking up in awe,
Colour fills the sky.

JOYS OF AUTUMN

Walking in
 crunchy leaves,
The smell of
 a bonfire
 somewhere
 nearby.

Wearing your favourite cosy jumper,
The sun hanging low in the sky.

Seeing pumpkins
 sitting on doorsteps,
Eating up warm
 yummy food.

The beautiful colours that dance all around
Can't help but put you in a good mood.

THINGS TO SEE IN AUTUMN

Blackberries growing

Spiderlings

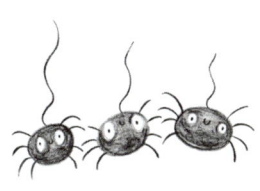

Colourful leaves

An acorn

A squirrel

A pumpkin

THINGS TO DO IN AUTUMN

Collect conkers.

Fly a kite on a breezy day.

Go for a walk in a forest.

Cosy up and read a book.

Eat yummy soup.

Visit a pumpkin patch.

AUTUMN WORDS

Crunchy

Crisp

Cosy

Misty

Harvest

Golden

AUTUMN DAYS

HALLOWEEN — a holiday often celebrated by dressing up, eating sweet treats and carving pumpkins.

HARVEST FESTIVAL — a celebration of the annual harvest. Often celebrated in schools and churches by giving donations of food to those in need.

MOON FESTIVAL — a Chinese festival held in the middle of autumn. Some of the festivities include displaying lanterns, spending time with family and eating traditional moon cakes.

BONFIRE NIGHT — a day where bonfires are lit and fireworks are set off to remember the Gunpowder Plot led by Guy Fawkes.

Winter

A SNOW DAY

We woke up one morning,
And the world was painted white.
The trees and the houses
  all covered in snow,
Much to our delight.

We got our hats and coats on,
Gloves and scarves too.
Then we ran into the garden,
There was so much to do!

First, we made snow angels,
Staring up at the snow filled sky,
Moving our arms to make our wings,
Fluffy flakes floating on by.

We built a happy snowman,
With a shiny pebble smile.
Then we ran inside for cocoa,
And to warm up for a while.

We went searching in the garage
To find our old red sledge,
And we whizzed around in circles,
Sometimes falling off the edge!

Then when the sun was sinking,
In the grey and heavy sky,
It was time to go inside,
We waved our snowman goodbye.

So many happy memories,
There was so much to do and play.
And we went to bed dreaming,
Of another snowy day.

A WINTER MORNING
(a haiku)

A winter morning,
The sun sunk low in the sky,
Misty, grey, skyline.

THE WINTER CHECKLIST

A big warm scarf
In your favourite colour.
A hat with a bobble on top.

A pair of mittens,
Tied together with string,
To keep your hands nice and warm.

A pair of socks,
The fuzzy kind.
Toasty toes inside your boots.

A jumper, a big one,
Comfy and cosy.
And a coat with a fluffy hood.

A COLD DECEMBER DAY

A blue and blurry skyline,
The sunshine sunken low.
Fluffy, furry, fuzzy clouds
Promise to give snow.

A crunchy carpet of crystal
That glitters in the sun.
A freezing frosty adventure
Can be the best of fun.

The bare, brown branches
stand silent and sway
In whistling winter winds
On a cold December day.

A LITTLE ROBIN

A little robin skipping.
They've come to say, "Hello!"
That robin seems to follow me
Everywhere I go.
Sometimes in my garden,
Sitting in the hedge.
That cheeky little robin,
Sometimes on my window ledge.
Their little eyes are shiny,
Their tummy red and rosy.
They fluff up all their feathers,
And settle down so cosy.

THE TREE

The lights, all aglow,
change the streets that you know,
Into a magical place for all.

The colourful orbs,
That climb to the top,
Of a tree standing green and tall.

Underneath
The many branches,
People gather round.

They sing
At the top of their voices,
A cheery and joyful sound.

The tree
Shines on above them,
A beacon for others to see.

They can come and join in,
If they'd like to.
Singing together under the tree.

LITTLE SNOWFLAKES

A little snowflake falls through the air,
It doesn't make a sound.
Perfectly fluffy and frosty and white,
It flutters down onto the ground.
You can't see it unless you look closer,
As tiny as snowflakes can be.
But each little snowflake is different,
Just like you and me.
No snowflake is quite like another,
Each one is one of a kind.
Each one is special, each one unique,
Like each one of us, a rare find.

THINGS TO SEE IN WINTER

Holly

Snowflakes

Ice

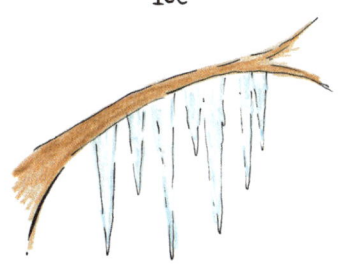

A robin

A pine tree

A snowman

THINGS TO DO IN WINTER

Drink hot chocolate with marshmallows.

Make some paper snowflakes.

Wrap up warm and go for a walk

Bake winter treats.

Build a snowman.

Build a den and read
your favourite book.

WINTER DAYS

THANKSGIVING — a holiday celebrated in America where people gather with family and show gratitude.

SNOW AND ICE FESTIVAL — a festival in China where people create ice sculptures to celebrate winter.

CHRISTMAS — a christian holiday to celebrate the birth of Jesus. It is celebrated in many countries by giving and receiving gifts and spending time with family.

THE WINTER OLYMPICS — a sporting ceremony held every 4 years in winter.

ABOUT THE AUTHOR

Kerri Cunningham, aka Murphy's Sketches, is a writer and artist from Preston in Lancashire. She lives in a small village with her husband and three children.

She has always loved drawing and writing and went to study Fine Art many years ago at UCLan. In recent years she has used her sketches and writing to bring some joy to people's day via her social media platform - Murphy's Sketches.

She writes a column for a local magazine each month called *Lancashire Life* where she talks about her experiences as a mum, and she works full time as an artist and writer selling cards and prints.

She loves to spend time outside with her family, and is so pleased to share her love of the outdoors and making the most of all the little things throughout the year in her first children's book *There is a Season*.

www.instagram.com/murphys_sketches
murphyssketches.co.uk